HANNIBAL'S ARMY
Carthage against Rome

ANDREA PRESS

Publishing Manager
César Álvarez

Editing
Carlos Canales

Published by
ANDREA PRESS
c/ Talleres, 21 - Pol. Ind de Alpedrete
28430 Alpedrete (Madrid)
Tel: 918 57 00 08 - Fax: 918 57 00 48
www.andrea-miniatures.com
andrea@andrea-miniatures.com

Photography
C. Canales: 5, 11, 15a, 17, 37a, 39, 40a, 41a, 46.
Corbis: 6, 7, 8, 9b, 11, 13a, 15b, 19a, 33, 36, 37b, 38
Prisma: 9a,
Aisa: 10, 12, 13b, 18a, 41b, 47
IGDA: 18b, 19b, 40b, 50
Oronoz: 32

Illustrations
David Jiménez (P-15)
Luis Leza

Translation:
Sally-Ann Hopwood

Corrections:
Charles P. Davis

Maps:
Wagram Imagen y Diseño
F. Castracane

Printed by
Gráficas Europa

Depósito Legal: S. 1.057-2005
ISBN 84-96527-57-3

INDEX

Between 264 BC and 146 BC, Carthage and Rome fought three long wars for the domination of the western Mediterranean. These wars have gone down in history as the Punic Wars. The fighting reached an epic scale for the time and such ferocity would not be repeated until modern times where both sides risked all their human and material resources as a means to achieve victory. When the wars ended, Carthage, previously known as the most beautiful western city, was in ruins, its' citizens dead or sold into slavery and its culture on the road to extinction. Her enemy, Rome, on the other hand, passed from being a purely Italian power to becoming the dominant force in the Mediterranean that would soon become Mare Nostrum.

Of the three wars, it was the second, fought from 218 to 202 BC, that has always attracted the public's imagination thanks to the stature of the commander-in-chief of the Punic Army: Hannibal. He was, and remains, arguably the finest tactician in the history of warfare whose epic march from Spain to Italy over the Alps is still considered to be a superhuman achievement for its time. This, combined with his three spectacular victories in open battle against the might of the Roman legions, has given Hannibal an honoured place among the great military leaders of all time. This controversial figure, whose personality and character inspired his army, caused the Romans to lay the overall blame for their overwhelming defeats on him. It is not surprising that the great historian Tito Livio, when called upon to give a name for what is now known as the Second Punic War, simply called it "Hannibal's War".

The Western Mediterranean around 220 BC. The loss of Sicily following the First Punic War (264-241 BC) and subsequent handing over of Sardinia and Corsica to Rome impelled the Carthaginians led by Hamilcar Barca to look towards Spain where, after three decades of fighting, they consolidated a strong position. By that time, Rome had defeated the last Gallic invasion at Telamon (225BC) and was already lord and ruler of Italy.

CARTHAGE

According to tradition, the legend goes that Carthage was founded in the 9th century BC or, more precisely 814 BC, by Phoenicians led by the legendary Queen Dido, or Elisa, emigrating from Tyre. It then gradually grew into an influential commercial empire that dominated the Western Mediterranean for over two hundred years, controlling both banks of the Columns of Hercules and navigation in the Atlantic Ocean. Confronted by the Greeks along the length of the Spanish coast, to which they gave the name Isspanya, the Land of the Rabbits, the Gauls and Italians settled firmly in Sicily, Sardinia, Corsica and the Balearic Islands, where they usually occupied, or built strongly fortified cities on the coast, maintaining only advanced commercial positions in the interior. Their constant confrontation with the Greeks led them to sign two treaties with Rome, when the city of Lacio was no more that a miniscule Italian state in permanent war with its neighbours, one in 508 BC and the other in 348 BC.

At the dawn of the third century BC, Carthage was probably the most beautiful city in the world; it enjoyed a formidable port and its ships navigated the principle commercial routes of the Oikumene (the known world) at their will. Exotic animals and wood arrived at the Punic port from inland Africa, cloth and luxury goods from Egypt and Asia, slaves and metals from the European Atlantic coasts. Carthaginian merchants reached the farthest distant points of the globe: legendary India, the Tin Islands and the Lands of Amber. Their war fleet was respected and feared and their mercenary armies, well armed and equipped, appeared to be sufficient to protect the metropolis from any attack. Although some of the aspects of their tradition seemed repulsive to the Greeks, such as those of the horrible cult of Moloch, which sacrificed children in honour of Baal Hammon, little by little, the Hellenic culture penetrated the Punic society, mainly via dress fashions, social customs and the army. In this city of merchants and sailors, the emotional impact induced by the Tyrant of Syracuse's attack on Agathocles in 310 BC, with its modern Macedonian style army against Carthage itself and the following war in Sicily against Pirro of Epiro, obliged the Carthaginians to consider the need to raise a land-based military force. They had a measure of success and, around 370 BC, became overseers of southern and western Sicily.

With respect to governance, the city was in the hands of a powerful oligarchy of merchants who controlled most of the territory around the city as well as maritime commerce. The land was highly fertile, much more so than modern Tunisia, and the cultivation methods were excellent and very modern. As well as the Carthaginian citizens, there was another elite class, dubbed Liby-Phoenicians by the Greeks that were the

View of Carthage with Dido and Eneras. Oil painting on canvas by Joseph Mallord William Turner

The Roman Ambassador, Quinto Fabius, at the moment of the declaration of war. Engraving.

product of a mixture of North African races. However, the remainder of the population did not have citizens' rights. Though the territory of Carthage was slightly greater than that of ager Romenus, the number of citizens was much lower.

Like Rome, Carthage originated from a monarchy. However, during the period of the Second Punic war, two annually chosen Shofets (judges) governed it. Wealth was as important as civil and political merit for attaining these positions and both judges held supreme civil and religious command, but not military. A counsel formed of thirty elders, gerousia, acted as a consultative organ and another tribunal, the Counsel of the One Hundred and Four, served as a supervisor to guarantee a kind of separation of powers, although this did not happen in practice. If the counsels could not agree, the Assembly of the People had the last word. The Greeks, like the great Aristotle, though bitter enemies of the Punic, praised their system of government that permitted the combination of elements from the old monarchies, the aristocracy and democracy, thus conferring on them a certain advantage by having more stable governments compared to the chaotic and unstable Hellenic city-states or the despotic monarchies successors of the Empire of Alexander the Great.

Views of the city of Carthage rebuilt for the Romans

THE PUNIC WARS

Historians down the ages have always been fascinated by the causes behind the great conflicts. The majority of modern researchers firmly believe that if any Roman or Carthaginian has been asked just one year before the start of the First Punic War about the possibility of a devastating conflict between both cities that was to last for more than a century and be made up of three frightful wars, they would have undoubtedly responded with great incredulity. The reason being that, until that moment, not only had there never existed a single reason for antagonism, but rather that Carthage and Rome had been friends.

Whatever the case, confronted by Carthage, the Romans acted as they usually did, pursuing the war through to its final consequences, which always concluded in the same way: total victory for the Romans. The Carthaginians that had lived in Sicily for decades perhaps thought that a war with Rome would simply be another war

like the confrontations that had taken place with other Western Mediterranean peoples over the centuries. Although this appears absurd today, the Carthaginian took an inordinately long time to discover their mistake. The truth being that there were many reasons to fear the Roman method of war. Shortly beforehand, Rome had been confronted for the first time by a Hellenic army, that of Pirro, a general so great that although he suffered two crushing defeats, he ended up winning and taking the last Italian Greek city, Taranto, in 272 BC. Its fighting and triumphant willpower and the relentless hardness of the legions had converted the Roman Army of the epoch into a terrible adversary, but the oligarchy of Carthage refused to acknowledge the obvious. After suffering surprising and hard-fought hand-to-hand defeats at sea against a inexpert Roman fleet equipped with new mechanical elements, such as the corvus, which compensated for its apparent inferi-

The Carthaginians and Romans at war during the First Punic War. In the beginning, the use of elephants was a crucial advantage for the Carthaginian army, but the Romans soon learned how to counteract them. Painting from the Raphael School, 1534-1549.

The surrender of Carthage meant the loss of commercial control over the area plus the payment of huge amounts of silver to their conquerors. Portrait of Scipio. oil painting by Federico Madrazo. San Fernando's School of Arts Royal Academy, Madrid, Spain.

ority, little by little, Carthage recovered. Its reconstructed army was capable of beating the Roman invaders in Africa and a series of naval victories and Roman disasters in storms returned the domination of the sea to Carthage, though it did nothing for 14 years. Its leaders were not aware of what they were playing with and let a great opportunity slip away. There was no help from Hamilcar's troops that were fighting in Sicily and after the Roman naval victory at the Aegates Isles in 241 BC, Carthage had no choice but to reach a peace agreement. Carthaginians were forced to evacuate Sicily, free their Roman prisoners and pay 2,200 Eubian talents in compensation to the Roman state over a period of 20 years.

In the year 238 BC, the Carthaginians were forced to abandon Sardinia, which although it cost the Romans a hard war against the Sardinians in the interior, meant a new humiliation for Carthage. The foundations for the new war were already laid.

Roman and Carthaginian warships in battle. In the centre can be seen the corvus that was used by the Romans to board an enemy ship. Early 20th Century illustration.

THE BARCA FAMILY

Hannibal's success would have been impossible without his family. His father, Hamilcar devotee of Melkart, played an important role during the First Punic War. He had been in charge of recruiting one of the mercenary armies that was to fight the Romans in Sicily. The complicated situation of the Carthaginian troops on the island required skilful and ingenious strategies and tactics that would organise them to stop the relentless Roman advance. With his mercenaries hired in the Balearic Islands and Iberian littoral (both Hannibal's wife and mother were originally from Ebyssos, now Ibiza), he landed in Sicily and after taking Hercita (Pellegrino), he attacked the fort of Erix (Erice) and maintained an ingenious position against the Romans. As stated earlier, confronted with a lack of help and understanding from the Carthaginian leaders, he was obliged to reach a peace agreement which effectively meant the defeat of Carthage and the loss of the island, although Rome later broke the Peace Treaty and forced the Carthaginians to also abandon Corsica and Sardinia.

Upon his return to Carthage, Hamilcar played a pivotal role in suppressing the mercenary rebellion that was about to put an end to the great city of Punic. His political and military skills were put to the test during these difficult years. However, he finally achieved peace although at great cost in terms of suffering.

The Second Punic War began when Hannibal Barca captured Sagunto. From there he crossed the Alps with his elephants and began the invasion of Italy. He was finally defeated at Zama in 202 BC. He escaped and took refuge in Bitinia where he committed suicide. Painting in the Uffizi Gallery, Florence, Italy.

As a consequence of the Mercenary War and the loss of the islands off the Italian peninsular, Hamilcar realised that for Carthage to survive, it would need to become more powerful, in order to one day return to challenge the Romans. He believed, with almost total certainty that the terrible Roman wolf would end up attacking Carthage again. He counted each year, month and even day while planning the strategy of how to survive and overcome the coming definite confrontation with the overlords of Italy. To do this, he set his sights on Spain, the legendary western land of which the Punic sailors related stories and legends. So, accompanied by a small army under his command and that of his son-in-law, Hasdrubal the Handsome, he landed at Cadiz, the main Punic city of Iberia, prepared to increase Carthage's power. Accompanying them was also his eldest son of just nine years old. He was called Hannibal.

As with all the Carthaginians, Hamilcar had been fascinated with Spain since childhood. Some legends tell that

Amilcar Barca, the Carthaginian leader during the First Punic War. He had to overcome many adversaries before he was able to return his city to its former glory. Engraving. National Library, Madrid, Spain.

he was born on the island of Cabrera, a land of immense riches yet to be explored, of gold mines, meadows full of livestock and inhabited inland by brutal 'white savages' with which to fill the mercenary armies to overflowing. With a mixture of ingeniousness, political intrigue and force, Hamilcar took control of the valley of Betis (Guadalquivir) and began to secure control of the coast. He later headed inland fighting against Iberian and Celtic people who he defeated after hard campaigns that toughened his army, gaining experience and skill. After the foundation of Akra Leuke, laid upon the remains of the ancient Greek foundry Hemeroskopeion (modern Alicante) and his nearing the Ebro (230 BC), the fear of the progressive expansion of Carthage made its way to Rome. At this time, it was involved in a brutal war with the Cisalpine Gauls and was in no condition to intervene, a fact of which the Punic leader took advantage to secure territory in his hands.

After his death in battle (229 BC) in Helike, for many authors the real Elche although others opine that it could have been Elche de la Sierra, in Albacete. This is somewhat more logical, given that he was in Oretani territory at the time and not that of his Mastienos allies. Command of the army passed to Hasdrubal, who continued with Hamilcar's policies.

During his rule, Hasdrubal founded the city of Cartagena, Qart-Hadasat or the New City, which would become the headquarters of the Carthaginian government in Spain. It was, and remains an excellent natural port that, today, is the principal Spanish naval base in the Mediterranean. He reinforced and improved the army so that it became a superb war machine of more than 70,000 men It was made up of mostly Hispanic mercenaries, to which must be added the Numidians constituting the light cavalry, the Liby-Phoenician Phalange, 6,000 horses and at least 200 heavy and medium elephants.

Rome was alarmed by the expansion of Carthage and insisted that it should neither cross the line of the Ebro nor threaten the Edetana city of Saguntum, ally of Massalia — Marseille. The murder of Hasdrubal by one of his Spanish servants after returning from a hunt (221 BC), apparently

Oil painting portraying the moment when Hannibal recognized his brother Asdrubal's head, killed by the Romans. Giovanni Battista Tiepolo. 1728-1730

an act of revenge, didn't stop the work of the Barca family that now had a successor capable of taking command. Despite his youth- he was 26 years old - Hannibal, by the grace of Baal, Hamilcar's son, who had accompanied his father and brother-in-law on their campaigns since he was a child, had already amply demonstrated his tactical skill and command capabilities. He was a robust youth, experienced in war and complex negotiations with tribes and was practically a Spaniard, for which the Iberian mercenaries and the old comrades of his brother-in-law and father adored him. Hence, even before confirmation of his command arrived from Carthage, the troops had already acclaimed him as their leader. The Punic expansion in Spain was to undergo a sudden, strong thrust under the iron command of its new leader.

Hannibal swore eternal hatred against the Romans. Lithograph from the 19th Century by J. Amigoni. According to tradition, the great Hamilcar Barca forced his eldest son to never forgive the humiliation inflicted upon his people by Rome.

HANNIBAL'S FIRST CAMPAIGNS

The new Carthaginian leader was a man of action. He was confident that the army would follow him. Unlike his brother-in-law, he was neither willing to employ delaying tactics nor to negotiate with the tribes more than was necessary. He had an experienced and loyal army and he was not prepared to leave it inactive. In the year that he gained command, while the Romans prepared to confront a new Gallic invasion of Italy, Carthage merely controlled the coast from the Algarve to Alicante and the valleys of Guadalquivir and Guadiana. Hannibal resolved to occupy the interior. To achieve this, he started a series of campaigns against the Olcades and the Carpetani, nowadays the Autonomous Community of Castile La Mancha, obtaining enormous riches after simple victories and carrying out acts of planned terror in order to eliminate resistance.

In 220 BC, he initiated a campaign that resumed the work successfully begun years ago. The objective was the subjection of the Vaccaei, a Celtic people living in the present day provinces to the north east of Castile and Leon, a place where the Punic army had never previously ventured. To avoid the tough and tenacious Carpetani, he left Sierra Morena, advancing along what later became known as the Silver Route, crossing Extremadura to reach Helmantika (Salamanca), which fell after a difficult battle. He continued advancing until reaching Toro but then retreated before the arrival of winter.

On his return, he had to fight armed groups of Olcaldes and Carpetani and, moreover, a large, tough but ill-disciplined Celt-Iberian army that ambushed him while retreating and crossing the Tajo, inflicting a terrible defeat upon him. He learnt this lesson well as this was the best style of tactics that he would use against the Romans in Italy.

By his the victory in the inland mountains and meadows, Hannibal achieved several things. He had established up to which point he could rely on his men, tested their discipline and fighting qualities and intimidated

The final day at Saguntum. Oil painting on canvas by Francisco Domingo Marqués

Archaeological medieval ruins of Roman walls of Sagunto, north of present-day Valencia.

the Celtic and Celt-Iberian tribes of the interior, revealing the strength of Carthage and demonstrating that it was better to be a friend of the Punic rather than their enemy. In consequence, the chiefs of warrior groups soon flocked to enlist alongside his men under the standard of the sun and half moon to fight for the invincible Carthaginian leader. The panorama in Spain had changed completely. All thought of rebellion had dissipated and the tribes knew who was Lord and Master of Spain. The great Hamilcar had a worthy heir.

At the beginning of 219 BC, Hannibal married Imilce, the daughter of the minor king of Castulo, with whom he had just one son, Aspar, of which very little is known. The Roman hatred and aversion of Carthage and Hannibal caused them to remove all trace of his memory; the legionaries even destroyed Imilce's grave when they occupied her the city of her birth.

Relief of an Osuna warrior in Seville, Spain. Short tunic, Celtic shield, falcata and hood. This warrior became the prototypical image of Hannibal's Spanish mercenaries. Men like him followed the Punic leader until the end.

SAGUNTUM

In 219 BC, the city of Saguntum (modern Sagunto), allied with Rome, attacked its Turdetan, Turboleta and Edetano neighbours. Strangely, the city was actually Edetana, but its urban design, commerce and growing prosperity had progressively isolated it from its neighbours. The economic tensions among the interior peoples, maliciously instigated by the Carthaginians, unfolded into fully-fledged armed conflict. The cause lay in the monopoly of commerce and exportation of the valuable iron weapons that the people of Saguntum acquired from the Turboletas and commercialised in the rich Masaliotas markets, who in turn exported them throughout Oikumene. The commerce of Saguntum notably prejudiced its neighbours, who were unable to compete with the vigorous Levantine city. Actually, Saguntum lay within the Carthaginian sphere of influence so, in principle, Rome should not have intervened. On the other hand, Hannibal, who had already decided to attack Italy, needed to secure the entire Spanish Mediterranean coast, as it would have been risky to leave the Romans occupying a friendly port. Resolved to put an end to the dangerous Saguntian independence, Hannibal placed the city under siege. The Punic tactician knew that it would be a difficult blockade, but couldn't have possibly imagined to what extent.

Built firmly on the River Palencia, the modern walls of Saguntum had been reinforced through a system of strongholds constructed according to the most advanced Hellenic techniques. With Masaliota assistance? Or perhaps Roman? The citizens had Spanish-type modern arms, which reveals that its troops were well trained. Confident in their impregnable positions, they prepared to confront the huge Punic army. Hannibal, although a great tactician, had enormous difficulties with the siege. He knew that the weakest point was on the western side and focused all his efforts there. He used artillery, scorpions and an intensive mining operation but, despite this, he couldn't breach the main walls. Meanwhile, the defender's fierce counter-attack sallies sapped the army's morale and, as if that were not enough, they received a Roman mission that threatened to break the siege. The Romans also tried to have them removed and if it hadn't been for the huge quantities of silver sent by Hannibal to buy influence in the Counsel it could, perhaps, have succeeded because in Carthage there were many oligarchs who were opposed to any confrontation with Rome.

Meanwhile, Carthaginian progress at the siege was minimal and, in addition, a filarial thrown by one of the defenders wounded the Carthaginian leader who returned to Carthage to recover from his injury. Finally, in October, he returned to the besieged city. The panorama greeting him was desolating. Little progress had been made, although the city was on the brink of surrender due to hunger wreaking havoc among the defenders. However, ghost-like, they maintained their positions. The city did finally fall into Hannibal's hands, but the lesson had been a bitter one. Throughout the Italian campaign, the great Punic leader avoided sieges whenever possible. It is also quite possible that the ghost of Saguntum came to mind in the days following Cannae, when he decided not to attack Rome, perhaps imagining the same problems as before the Iberian city but amplified to gigantic proportions. If this was what really happened, and it is very likely, the Roman world was eternally indebted to the valiant defenders of that small Edetana city, who preferred to die at their posts rather than surrender.

Over time, Saguntum was to become one of the myths of 19th Century Spanish romantic history, in which the authors of the period believed they saw the qualities of "self-sacrifice and resistance" in their fellow citizens. Obviously, at the time it was no more than a defence to the death of an isolated community that probably believed, until the very last moment, that they would receive help from Rome or their ally, Marseille.

An Olcade and a Mastieno warrior prepare themselves to storm an opening in Saguntum, while a slinger prepares to assist them by firing his deadly weapon. The Celtic or Iberian origin of the Olcaldes is still under debate even today. They lived in Cuenca, part of Teruel, part of Alicante and Ciudad Real; their panoply is valiant and warlike, as was usual for the region and period, a mixture of Indo-European and Iberian origin. Their small shield, the caetra, is prominent, as is their efficient falcate. In the centre, in a dark woollen smock, is a Mastieno, inhabitant of Murcia, the Iberian people who supplied some of Hannibal's most noted warriors. His hood, another of the features described by historians such as Estrabon as being typical of the people of the region. He is also carrying a falcate and a caetra. Finally, on the right, is a Balearic slinger. They were trained from childhood to reach such precision with their shots that they could match any archer. They used various types of slingshots of different calibre and type of projectiles.

THE CARTHAGINIAN ARMY

After the wars against Agathocles of Syracuse and Pirro of Epiro, the Carthaginian tacticians had to confront for the first time what was then understood to be a modern army, one constructed according to the model imposed by Philip and Alexander the Great of Macedonia. Although the Carthaginians resisted successfully, it is also a fact that they showed serious weaknesses when confronting troops organised in the Hellenic style. Formed by men trained in the complex use of long lances (of the Phalange) and to act in a coordinated way with the rest of the Phalange and the cavalry, the Hellenic armies were composed of free citizens that lived in permanent military colonies. They were effective, disciplined and highly prepared, but replacing any losses was not easy.

Furthermore, the battles between the successive kingdoms of Alexander the Great, all equipped with similar armies, had produced an intense arms race throughout the 3rd Century BC It was an ongoing search to gain

Coin minted in Carthage, representing a horse and a palm tree, and dated during the first years of Hannibal's command, around 220 BC. The symbols most identifiable with North Africa were those commonly used by the people of Carthage.

Ceramic vase from an archaeological excavation at San Miguel de Liria, Spain. Depicted on it can be seen two Iberian warriors like the ones recruited by Hannibal for his mercenary army.

any advantage when similarly matched enemies met, given that war had been transformed into a mirror image confrontation. It was not unusual to see the appearance of linen cuirasses reinforced with metal elements, chariots, falcados, chain mail, cuirassed elephants and any new element that might provide some small but significant advantage on the battlefield.

In this sense, the Carthaginian reforms were very slow. The number of citizens was comparatively very small and, in consequence, recruiting was low. So, it became necessary to permanently resort to the use of mercenaries. Furthermore, to equip and maintain a Hellenic type army was very expensive. Not only for the quality of material required: swords, lances, helmets, cuirasses, greaves, etc., but also because constant training was required. So, even though the wealth and power of Carthage increased, its army was still little more than a force made up of foreigners, not only the warriors and sub-commanders but sometimes even the campaign troop generals, such as the Spartan mercenary Xanthippe. It was he who organised and adapted the antiquated and scarcely operational

Hellenic-style helmet. National Archaeological Museum, Madrid. It is of the type most commonly used by senior Roman officers and Punic soldiers. It was discovered in Spain and awarded an erroneous identification as it is catalogued as a Roman helmet. It has no feather-holder or support for the Italian-style mane so is, almost certainly, a helmet belonging to a Carthaginian soldier.

Carthaginian army at the beginning of the First Punic War, converting it into a modern, efficient force capable of confronting the Regulus legions. These had landed in Africa and were beaten on the banks of the Bagradas River, the first open battlefield victory of a Carthaginian army over a Roman one (255 BC).

Throughout this period, the Carthaginian army recruited soldiers from many diverse origins. Most notable was the permanent recruitment of light cavalry from their Numidian neighbours and, at least from the 4th Century BC, from Iberians and other people from the Iberian Peninsular of which traces can be found in Sicily. To these, the Greeks, Italians and Gauls were later added. What is most surprising is that Carthage never tried, at least not after the Xanthippe reforms, to integrate them into a coherent combat scheme. Rather, each contingent fought using its own culture's arms and national style. In theory, this state of affairs should have created enormous problems but, incredibly, Hannibal managed to transform this into one of his main weapons when confronting the Roman legions.

Hannibal's army units were normally organised according to the nationality of origin, in order to take advantage of the virtues of each. This was particularly important for the troops of Hispanic or Gallic origin,

An Etruscan warrior. He is equipped in the Greek style, with a round shield and linen cuirass of the type used by the Carthaginian Phalange. Sarcophagus of the Tarquinian Amazons, Florence.

because they maintained intact their tribal structure, so that the warriors could fight as if they were defending their own people. From this, we know that Hannibal organised his mercenaries extremely intelligently, thus counting on balanced contingents of light and heavy infantry, cavalry and even elephants.

Given that Carthage usually had plenty of money, recruiting troops was easy, enabling the hiring of high quality recruits, carefully selecting each one for hid individual qualities, weaponry, physical state and even experience. In this sense, Hannibal was extremely rigorous and, at the onset of a campaign, he preferred not to use the 'unsafe' groups and retain only the most efficient and loyal. Furthermore, there was another drawback, the need to train and prepare very different groups to act in unison, a property for which the Carthaginian armies were a scarce and highly valued attribute; it was difficult to substitute his soldiers for an equivalent force. Perhaps this fact explains why the Punic commanders were less aggressive than their Roman counterparts, as they knew they could rely on excellent resources formed from well-armed and trained soldiers.

With respect to command of the army, as stated earlier the judges were not military commanders, so gen-

The Numidian cavalry was a very important element in Hannibal's army due to their great fighting qualities. Trajan's Column, Rome, Italy.

erals were appointed and allowed to operate until their dismissal. Traditionally, the Carthaginians gave out cruel, brutal treatment to any defeated general and it was not unusual for them to be crucified following a defeat, as they were held personally responsible for the losses. Some cases are known of crucifixion for simply failing to agree, or for refusing to confide in their senior officers. However, following the First Punic War, this radical practice became outmoded and Hannibal knew how to meet with his most trusted subordinates. One of his greatest merits was in knowing how to wait. By tradition, it was known that the greater time that units of diverse origins served together, the better they fought and adapted themselves to the orders and instructions of their Punic chiefs. The tough campaigns of Hamilcar, Hasdrubal and even Hannibal himself in the mountains and plateaus of interior Spain produced a fighting force of extraordinary quality that would form the basis for the campaign army that Hannibal led into Italy in

Heavy Punic infantryman and cavalryman. Generally, the Carthaginians used their own citizens as the shock troops. The light cavalry and light infantry were generally composed of Numidian and Hispanic mercenaries respectively.

A re-enactment group recreating a Celtic attack. The Gauls were among the most important contingents following the Carthaginian general once they had traversed the Alps.

218 BC. Up to the taking of Saguntum, Hannibal was able to forge a military force of such efficiency and cohesion that it surpassed anything that had ever been seen before in Carthage. The command structure reached a very high level, which enabled his army to first absorb thousands of Gauls and later Italians of diverse origins: Samnite, Lucanian, Sabelicos, Brutii, Umbrios and many more, losing neither quality nor efficiency. This is even more incredible when it is considered that the orders were transmitted in Punic and must have later been translated into the languages spoken by the different national groups of which the army was formed.

The downside of this, however, was that each operational Carthaginian army was unique and depended completely on its recruits and their capability, on the troops that could be found, on their training and their ability to integrate themselves into the group. For these reasons, armies of different origins and diverse compositions failed when they were obliged to cooperate with each other. This is what happened to Hannibal at Zama, where he had recruited three different types of troops on different occasions and had no time to make them into a cohesive whole.

Terracotta figure representing a Greek elephant with tower.

19

THE AFRICANS: CARTHAGINIANS AND LIBY-PHOENICIANS

The existence of a large contingent of citizens was one of the problems that Hannibal had to deal with when building his army. However, one important group of citizens with full rights from Carthage, the Spanish colonies and North Africa always formed a part of his army. Also, most of the senior commanders accompanying him on his campaigns came from this group.

The Africans were usually divided into two groups that, by the close of the 3rd Century BC, were effectively one and the same. The first, the Carthaginians came from the mother country or adjacent areas that formed part of the Tunisian Republic. They were, like the Romans, mostly land-owning country folk in what was then one of the most fertile zones of the world, a real paradise full of small forests, agriculture and livestock exploitation, all maintained by slaves. They were generally men that had received an acceptable level of education and had thorough, intensive training. They were hardened by desert campaigns against looting Numidians, or campaigns carried out by the Barca family in Spain and constituted an essential part of the nucleus of the Punic army. Together with them, there were some merchants, although it is known that they preferred the fleet, and the Liby-Phoenicians, as the Greeks called them, who were simply the result of the progressive mixing of the Punic colonies with the North African inhabitants. The Liby-Phoenicians were by then totally integrated into the Punic culture and constituted the greater part of the population of the Carthaginian coastal cities of northern Africa. In fact, they were still the majority population in the initial Roman epoch, in what today constitutes the province of Almeria and parts of Malaga y Murcia.

Considering their evident link with the expansionist policy of Hamilcar Barca and that of his successor Hasdrubal, for Hannibal, they constituted the main nucleus of his army.

Equipped and trained in the Hellenic style, at first glance they would have been indistinguishable from a Greek army. They fought in a Phalange, protected by round or oval shields, linen cuirasses, helmets and greaves and armed with Greek swords and long lances. They also formed the heavy cavalry, were well trained and disciplined, armed with Macedonian-style long Greek lances and swords and had cuirasses and helmets. During Hannibal's time, they protected the front part of the horses with metal scale armour of bronze or iron, which would provide the Carthaginian horsemen with excellent protection against the arrows, darts and javelins that tended to be used by Iberian and Celt-Iberian tribes.

It is still not known today how the Libyan light infantry units were formed. Recruitment was probably carried out in the Carthaginian cities along the coast and interior of Africa and Spain, from volunteers and, perhaps, by forced conscription from among the country folk working on the large farms.

The figure with the banner is a Carthaginian officer. He is wearing a Greek linen cuirass and a late Hellenic-style helmet. Although, according to British historian Peter Conolly, the most widely known emblem of Carthage is that of the disc and half moon, the version chosen is that described by the Spanish researcher José Antonio Alcaide, based on the coin represented on Page 16. Hannibal appears equipped in the ancient style, with a muscle-toned bronze cuirass. These cuirasses continued to be used by both Rome and Carthage even after the advent of chain mail, perhaps due to their lighter weight or because of tradition. In Rome, senior officers used them until the end of the Empire, but they were also used by legionaries and in a higher proportion than experts are willing to admit. The situation was somewhat similar in Carthage. Finally, the central figure is a Liby-Phoenician phalangist, armed in the Macedonian style that dominated the whole of the civilised Mediterranean, but with chain mail, an element from Carthage that was already being used before the Second Punic War, although admittedly on a very small scale. After the Battle of Lake Trasimene, Hannibal ordered his troops to use Roman chain mail, which was much sturdier than their linen armour.

THE AFRICANS: NUMIDIANS

The Numidians formed an essential part of the Carthaginian army for decades. The Carthage troops' senior commanders always liked to count on their help and devastating efficiency. They were recruited from the large, solitary neighbouring territories of Carthage in present day Tunisia and Argelia. They were brave, tough and aggressive, mounted on their small horses without saddles, bridles or bits; they wore simple tunics and were armed with javelins, protecting themselves with small round shields.

Although, at first glance, they appear to be excessively light, un-armoured cavalry, they were certainly aggressive. During Hannibal's campaign in Italy, led by their own tribal leaders and the great Mutines, the Carthaginian cavalry's finest commander, they proved to be distinctly superior to the Roman cavalry and her allies with respect to reconnaissance and also in battle. They were experts at ambush, they adapted marvellously to the Punic tactic of tricking the opposing commanders time and again. They fought, taking advantage of the speed and agility of their small horses, and closed with their enemy, harassing them with darts and javelins They would then turn away and give the impression that they were retreating, then surprise their pursuers once they had reached favourable ground, a method of fighting similar to that of the later torna fuya of the Spanish Middle Ages.

Although the only available reliable representation of Numidian horsemen postdates the period when Hannibal lived by more than two hundred years, their clothing and mode of fighting probably hadn't change in all those years. However, the horses with which they appear depicted on the Trajan Column are too large, as it is now known that the horses from North Africa in Hannibal's time were not much larger than ponies, which perhaps explains why they used them in battle the way they did.

After the majority of the Numidians joined forces with the Romans late in the war, in 204 BC their leader, Masinissa, allied with Scipio and, particularly following the end of hostilities, and after Hannibal fled Carthage, his kings' ambitions turned against the interests of his protecting city. Little by little, they sequestered land from the Carthaginians, like removing the leaves from a lettuce. A defensive Carthaginian act provoked a terrible Roman reaction and, with it, the Third Punic War in 149 BC, which finally spelt the end of Carthage. After the war, the Romans were forced to confront the Numidians who, under the inspired leadership of the great king, Jugurtha, were a formidable enemy.

The Numidian horseman on the left is based on representations on the Trajan Column. Although it shows men at the beginning of the 2nd Century AD, it represents the efficient North Africans as they were in those years, having changed very little, if at all, from their ancestors who fought in the Punic wars. The only harness is a cord around the horse's neck that could serve as an occasional holding point. Next to him, there is a dismounted Numidian with his sheaf of javelins. In the Italian wars, the behaviour of the African light horsemen was admirable and at Cannae they collaborated with the Gallic and Hispanic cavalries with great efficiency in the annihilation of the enemy army.

The man appearing next to the Numidians is a mahout, an elephant driver. In principle, they originated from Asia, where the use of pachyderms as a weapon of war began, which is why the riders, perhaps originating from some distant Asian peninsular were denominated 'Indians'. However, it is known that they were mostly Africans. They were armed with a tool that served to kill the beast should it go berserk, which happened often, as the animals were terribly unstable on the battlefield.

THE SPANISH: IBERIANS, CELTS AND CELT-IBERIANS

Undoubtedly, Hannibal, in spite of his ability and genius, would not have been able to carry out the incredible adventure of invading Italy, nor would he have had any of the victories that were to turn him into legend, had it not been for the help, cohesion and even fanatical adhesion of his Spanish warriors. Born into a society that glorified military success and warlike abilities, the Iberian fighters are undoubtedly among the most deadly warriors in history. They were tough and audacious with demonstrable bravery and, although it is sometimes overlooked, they were excellently armed and equipped; they were to be the real backbone of Hannibal's army, even more so than the Carthaginians themselves. During preparations for the Italian campaign, Hannibal's agents recruited warriors from hundreds of tribes, some located farther afield than the most remote places where the Punic had been, but who had heard about a young invincible leader and his powerful army and they were keen for spoils, adventure and glory.

The Iberians that lived along the Levantine coast up to the modern day French Provence, had centuries of experience in contact with the great cultures of the Mediterranean. Their leather and bronze helmets, high crests, short swords and lethal javelins were known, valued and feared throughout the old world, as they had frequently fought as mercenaries in Greek and Carthaginian armies. Many of their cities had already reached an acceptable level of development, although not as high as that of the Betica cities, and their warriors were used to the fighting style of the best armies of the era.

The Celts, the product of waves of invaders from Northern and Central Europe that had penetrated the Iberian Peninsula for centuries were the dominant people in the centre and west. Finally, there were the Celt-Iberians, generally dubbed the Indo-European people who had settled in Spain having had more intensive contact with the South-Eastern Iberians and had reached a kind of cultural synchronicity.

Traditionally, Roman historians classified the Spanish warriors as light infantry, called caetrati, formed of warriors armed with small, round shields, short swords and several javelins, and the heavy infantry or scutati, armed with lances and swords and protected with large shields, helmets and cuirasses. The Spanish infantry was not made up of simple hordes of disordered, ill-disciplined warriors with a single purpose. It consisted of skilled and able warriors that emanated from cultures that had already had years of experience of the most modern methods of warfare and whose ancestors had fought against experienced armies. From analysing and studying ancient classics and studies undertaken by contemporary specialists such as José María Cagigal and José

Antonio Alcaide, it is demonstrable that the warriors of ancient Iberia were capable of confronting the all-powerful Roman legionaries on the open battlefield on equal terms, something that was within the reach of very few ancient people. Hannibal's admiration for his Spanish soldiers is not surprising, neither is the important role played by them throughout the course of the war.

In the 3rd Century BC, the intense commercial and war contact between the diverse peoples of the Iberian Peninsula had provoked what can be looked upon as the logical regional and cultural differences, of typically Hispanic weaponry, to the extent that classical researchers can easily distinguish the Iberian Peninsula warriors from those from other parts of the Mediterranean world. Perhaps, the uniformity of the Greco-Roman world dress of which historians speak: white or crudely coloured tunics, trimmed with purple, were no more than a convention, although it is possible that Hannibal had tried to give some kind of uniformity to his warriors. This would never be as perfect as that represented by some historians, because the tribes almost certainly retained the arms and costume first of their nation and then, as do all warriors, taking whatever they could from their enemies.

To the left, a Turdetan warrior can be seen in the classic reconstruction by Peter Conolly and José A. Alcalde, dressed in a bone-coloured tunic with a crude red border (purple was very expensive), and a hood like that of the Osuna warriors. His Celtic shield is large and he is armed with a falcate, the most beautiful weapon of the ancient world. In the centre is a warrior typical of one of the peoples of central or western Spain, who could be Lusitanian, Carpenati, Celtic or Oretani. He wears a woollen tunic and carries a lance and round shield. Round his neck, he wears a torque, one of the symbols of the Indo-European warriors. For some historians, the Lusitanians, whose leader, Viriato, would make his grand entrance onto world history half a century later, were a superposition of Ligurians, Iberians, Lucanian and Celts, the family to which their language belonged. Finally, on the right, is a Vaccaei warrior of the Celtic tribe that fought Rome for the longest period of time and was not totally defeated until the time of Emperor Augustus in the year 26 BC. The warrior is armed with a La Tene III type Celtic sword, a weapon that was widespread throughout Central Europe. He is wearing a Montefortino type helmet, similar to that of the Roman legionaries, of which various specimens have been found in Spain. The use of trousers, bragas, is noteworthy. The shield and lance are typically Celtic.

If the participation of the Spanish warriors in Hannibal's army was essential because of their quality, the Gauls were essential for their numbers. After the epic Alpine crossing and once Gallic Cisalpine had been reached, Hannibal could rely on thousands of spirited and strong warriors willing to fight under his standards. Later, having so many available recruits, he could choose the most capable. It was sometimes said that Hannibal scorned the Celts: "forraje para el pilum", whom he undoubtedly considered to be strong men, physically well built for war, but impetuous, unstable and not very thoughtful. Like the Romans, he knew that the charge of the barbarian European tribes was fearful due to the violence and impetuousness of their warriors, but if one knew how to contain them, it was then relatively simple to break their lines and organise a real butchery. Perhaps for that reason, he used the Gaul warriors that fought in his lines as authentic 'cannon fodder', as he was aware that they were easily replaced, whereas his Spanish mercenaries and African Phalanges were irreplaceable.

The Gauls were the product of centuries of invasions from the west and south of Europe by people from Indo-European origins, who came from the centre of the continent moving slowly in several waves, to the west, east and south, reaching the British Isles, the Iberian Peninsula and even modern day Turkey; the galatas. The Gauls are usually linked with the La Tene culture, one of the main Celtic cultures, and had been present in Italy since the great invasions at the beginning of the 4th Century BC. During one such invasion, a strong warrior group under the command of an able chief, Breno, made short work of a Hoplite army of the Roman Republic at Allia (390 BC), taking and looting Rome itself. The Romans soon recovered, but throughout the century, the Italian Peninsular suffered an avalanche of wave after wave of Gauls, something that influenced the decisive collapse of the Etruscan culture. It affected the forms of war and weaponry of the Italian people, who adopted many elements of Celtic armament, such as the most widely used helmet of the Punic Wars, the so-called Montefortino type and chain mail It also provoked radical changes in their own weaponry, in order to better confront armed bands of Gauls that, on more than one occasion, raided as far south as the wheat fields of Campania, in Italy's deep south. The last invasion ended in catastrophic defeat against the Romans at Telamon (225 BC), and the Roman counter-attack that finished with the brutal and bloody occupation of Gallic Cisalpine. The conquest was not complete nor was the region totally pacified when Hannibal's troops landed in Italy in 218 BC. It is hardly surprising that the humiliated, fierce and beaten Gauls joined in their masses those who had come to free them. This cost Rome another fierce battle, after Hannibal's defeat, to recover the territory that had been lost. During the following centuries, Rome destroyed the Celtic people systematically in Gaul, Britain and Hispania, until almost completely eliminating their culture and language so that, today, only small remnants remain in Wales, Ireland and Brittany.

The Gauls fought by charging headlong against the enemy in the hope of breaking their lines upon the first impact. They were tall, strong men who impressed the Mediterranean people with their demeanour and fearlessness. However, it did not take long for the Mediterraneans to figure out how to fight them, their superior organisation and training gave them a decisive advantage.

On the left is a typical Gallic Cisalpine warrior. His weaponry is that typically used by the La Tene culture: a very large shield, a bronze helmet and long sword, with a blade length of up to 60 cms. These swords were better than is usually said of them and can be found throughout Western Europe. They were cutting weapons that became progressively longer over time and were used to land devastating blows on the enemy. At Telamon, some Gallic tribes still fought almost naked, in the old style but, over time, the Gallic armies adopted better protection. The chief in the centre is a war leader from a unit inducted into Hannibal's heavy infantry. For protection he carries a shield and wears a helmet and heavy chain mail made of iron links, the most exotic armour in history and invented by the Gauls at the beginning of the 3rd Century BC. The wealthiest legionaries began using chain mail during the First Punic War and by the beginning of the Second it was already widespread. Finally, on the right, is a Gallic horseman with his round shield and heavy armour. The Roman cavalry later adopted the saddle equipped with horns.

THE MEN WHO FOUGHT IN THE SECOND PUNIC WAR (218-202 BC)

Carthaginian Officer. He wears the typical Hellenic panoply of the Macedonian type as used by the Punic since their first war against Rome. The cuirass is of linen: flexible, but not very protective. On his back is a shield with the two components of the Phalange.

Carthaginian Soldier. This sentinel from a fortified place in Spain carries no shield and instead of the long lance of the Phalange warriors, he has a shorter weapon, more useful for his mission. He is protected by a bronze-scaled cuirass, which is very efficient but quite expensive and not very flexible.

Carthaginian Soldier. After the first victories in Italy, principally after Lake Trasimene, Hannibal ordered his men to use the magnificent chain mail of the legionaries that, though heavy, offered greater protection. At Cannae, the men of the Carthaginian Phalange were indistinguishable from many of the enemy.

Carthaginian Standard Bearer. This horseman is also heavily armed. He is wearing the emblem of Carthage and, although protected by a round shield, he is also wears a solid-scale, oriental-type cuirass.

Gallic Chief. A Cisalpine warrior dressed in the famous checked material and armed with a long sword of the La Tene III type, common to all the Celtic tribes of Central Europe.

Gallic Warrior. This man may be a simple barbarian warrior, but his arms and armour were the envy even of his enemy, the Romans. Great smiths, the Gauls invented chain mail and even the Romans copied their helmets.

Gallic Warrior. In contrast to the previous illustration, this warrior was not wealthy enough to afford chain mail and protects himself with just a large shield. However, his long sword allows him to fight in closed lines.

Gallic Warrior. In this case, the Celtic warrior has a heavy ash or oak lance, a weapon uses throughout the west and also highly valued in Spain, where the northern people used very similar ones. His pointed helmet is one of the most ancient models that were rarely ever used by the time of the Punic Wars.

Edetano Warrior. This is a reconstruction of one of the warriors depicted on the vessel of San Miguel de Liria. He is well protected by his leather and bronze or iron scale cuirass and Celtic type shield and armed with a lethal falcate.

Celt-Iberian Warrior. The classic image of Hannibal's mercenaries, this Arevaco warrior is not very different from his distant relatives, the Gauls, because he has partly equipped himself with non-Hispanic weapons. The La Tene long swords appear in tombs and discoveries across Spain. However, they are quite rare and were probably imported, such as occurred with the first chain mail. His bronze helmet also originates from the other side of the Pyrenees.

Turdetan Warrior. He is directly inspired by Osuna's sculpture and the classical author's descriptions of Hannibal's Spanish soldiers. He wears a white, or rather crudely coloured tunic, trimmed in red over which is a fibre cloak decorated with a chimera with its mane dyed red. His shield is of the Celtic type and his sword the legendary falcate.

Lusitanian Warrior. Reconstructed according to the traditional image, with a short sword and dagger, this warrior is the spitting image of the ferocious fighters of the Central and Western European tribes. He is dressed in a heavy woollen tunic and armed with a Celtic lance and round shield.

Numidian Horseman. Mounted on their small horses, they were capable of galloping for days on end, dressed in simple tunics and only protected by their round leather shields. He is carries neither sword nor dagger.

Numidian Warrior. Without horses, the Numidian light javelin or dart throwers could inflict little damage on a well-protected and organised infantry. Hence, the horse was an essential element of their form of combat.

Lucan Warrior. The people of Central and Southern Italy shared a common culture and had developed similar weaponry. This warrior carries two light javelins and is protected with a Samnite-type shield and a Greek helmet with evidence of Celtic influence.

Samnite Warrior. Bitter enemies of the Romans, upon whom they inflicted some major defeats, their weaponry, as far as we know, was quite light and shared some similarities with that of the Romans. Skilled at setting ambushes and mountain warfare, the Samnites met with problems whenever they had to confront the Roman legions on the open battlefield.

THE ELEPHANTS

There are written records going back for at least 3000 years that illustrate the use of elephants in India as weapons of war. However, the use of elephants for military purposes in Hellenic culture is more recent. The introduction of war elephants in the western world dramatically took place on the banks of the River Hydaspes, in India, when Alexander the Great confronted King Porus's army in 326 BC. In this great battle, the Macedonian tactician faced over a hundred cuirassed elephants that, at times, managed to open gaps in the phalange. Admiring them for the use that could be made of these animals within his army, he captured some specimens in battle and added many others that he received as gifts from Indian princes, enabling him to possess over two hundred pachyderms at the time of his death. During the wars following the death of Alexander the Great, some of his generals enriched their armies with elephants, believing that due to their size and weight, they would become the decisive weapon of battle. In fact, King Seleucus I incorporated more than five hundred elephants in his powerful and modern army, which was probably the strongest army in the world at that time. The Seleucids were not the only Hellenic kings to equip their armies with elephants; Macedonians, Egyptians and Epirotas, began to train special riders and troops to fight mounted on elephants. During these years, at the end of the 4th Century BC and beginning of the 3rd, the Greek Oriental kings came up with even more sophisticated tactics, facilitating the efficient use of war elephants in the disciplined Hellenic armies. The Seleucids, for example, revealed compact lines of armoured and protected elephants in closed blocks that they then launched at the enemy lines until they were destroyed. These elephant 'blocks' were ably assisted by armed light infantry with bows and catapults. Each squadron consisted of one elephant, its rider, two crewmembers and forty back-up soldiers.

During the first decades of the 3rd Century BC, it was thought that the elephant was not only a necessary weapon, but also an essential part of modern warfare, hence other non-Hellenic armies of the Oikumene influenced by the powerful Greek culture gradually incorporated elephants into their armies. One of these states was Carthage that, furthermore, greatly influenced the tactical use of these great beasts.

The Indian elephants used in war were basically of the genus Elephas maximus, a gigantic animal between 2.5 and 3 metres tall and 5.5 to 6 metres long, weighing almost 5 tons and capable of carrying a heavy tower with an armed crew. Nearly all the Hellenic kingdoms tended to progressively cuirass their elephant to afford them better protection. This was because, after a century of battlefield use, almost all the armies had developed some kind of tactic to combat them.

Both the Egyptians and the Carthaginians looked for ways to avoid dependence on the Asian markets for obtaining elephants. The routes of communication with Asia were long and were almost always in enemy hands. They directed expeditions into the heart of Africa to capture specimens of Loxonta africana oxyotis, the savannah elephant, a colossal beast of up to 4 metres high to the withers with a weight frequently exceeding 6 tons and measuring up to 7.5 metres long. The great advantage of these monsters was that they could carry heavy towers with three crewmembers and more weapons, not only missile weapons, but also sarissas, the terrible 6 metre long phalange spears. They were captured in Sudan and from there they could be sent north along the length of the Nile without having to cross the Sahara Desert. The Carthaginians even managed to capture a specimen from Southern Tunisia that, today, is an extremely arid region.

However, there is also another type of elephant that was used extensively during the wars between Carthage and Rome, Loxonta africana cyclotis, or forest elephant. The Carthaginians caught them mainly in the Atlas forests not far from their capital. 2000 years ago, these forests, like the Guir forest in Morocco (now a desert), was then inhabited by all kinds of animals including lions, zebras and giraffes. These elephants were unable to carry a tower and were ridden by just one rider and another man armed with javelins and a bow. Hannibal took this species to Italy but although savannah elephants are repeatedly depicted fighting against the Romans at Trebia and Lake Trasimene, this never really occurred.

The elephants of Carthage had strong towers with a crew of three that formed an adequate team for their mission. The first, the mahout, or driver, was normally a Numidian, at least up until the battle of Zama, when the Numidians fought on the Roman side. This greatly affected the Carthaginian army that, in consequence, had to hire Indian riders with little or no military experience that undoubtedly was a cause of the terrible driving of the elephants during the battle. The rider sat behind the head, protected by the ears. He carried a type of pick with which to beat the animal if it went berserk. Then there were three men, an officer, an archer and a lancer or spearman armed with a long Hoplite lance. All three were dressed in heavy armour.

In spite of their imposing appearance, the elephants were mentally unstable, as the fire and deafening noise drove them mad, a situation which transformed them into beasts just as dangerous for friend and foe alike. Despite this, they continued to be used for military purposes in the Mediterranean until the beginning of modern times.

In February 218 BC, Hannibal visited the temple of Melkart in Cadiz. As the legend goes, the omens were favourable for the immediate future… but not for the far one. In any case, it was to be the last time that he would see his family; the dice were thrown. After taking Saguntum, the Carthaginian army leaders realised that they had to join forces after the spring. Rome had declared war on Carthage and the legions given orders to prepare for war. However, although time was of an essence, Hannibal would have preferred to let his troops rest and re-equip after the winter. A plan was brewing in his mind, a project so audacious that it would capture the men's imagination. He would go against the Romans, not in the way that they were expecting, but rather on their own land, on their own soil, in Italy. And of all the alternatives available, Hannibal decided for one that surpassed the imaginable: he would cross the Alps with his army.

Perhaps the project to attack Italy was an ancient one and it would be surprising if Hamilcar Barca himself had not planned to do it years before. To seek out the routes, prepare maps and make contact with the tribes must have been an enormous task that would certainly have taken years of work. Merchants, travellers and spies must have informed the Barca family leaders and destiny chose Hannibal, a military genius, to actually carry out the plan.

After ensuring backup by sending Iberian troops to Carthage and Numidians and Liby-Phoenicians to Spain, he prepared his men for a decisive confrontation. The army he left in Iberia was well equipped and reinforced to overcome any indigenous rebellion or Roman attack. His half brother Hasdrubal was left in charge.

The nucleus of selected troops headed north in the direction of the Ebro under the cover of intense spring rainfall. After overcoming Ilergete armed opposition, the

Hannibal crossing the Alps to reach Italy. A fresco by Ripanda from the 16th. Century.

expedition troops crossed the river in the middle of July over a pontoon bridge and advanced along the coast under harassing attacks from the regional tribes. The small Greek cities and trading posts, such as Ampurias, gave up without a fight and, seemingly, everything was proceeding according to plan. Everything, that is, until the army reached the Pyrenees, when the Carpetani decided that they would go no further than the "mountains of ice". Faced with the increasing intranscedence of other tribes, Hannibal decided after a war counsel with his generals and tribal leaders, to retain only his most loyal men and to send the remainder to Cartagena or leave them stationed in occupied positions in Catalonia. Given what these men achieved in the Alps and, later, in Italy, it was an inspired decision.

In total, Hannibal was left with 50,000 infantry, 10,000 horsemen and all the elephants.

There are numerous representations showing how Hannibal and his army crossed the mountain range. These two engravings show the enormous hardships the Carthaginians had to overcome in order to achieve in their historic goal.

ROME FACED WITH THE PUNIC PLANS

Of course, the Romans were aware of the possibility of a land attack, although they were confident in the superiority of their legions to face such an occurrence. There were basically three projects that the Romans had analysed:

1. The first of the possible attacks was a Carthaginian landing in southern Italy to try to unite the coastal Greeks, along with the Campania and Samnite people under arms, perhaps with the assistance of some kind of diversionary manoeuvre against Sicily or Sardinia.
This plan was reproduced to some degree in Pirro's pro-

ject. This was to seek the alliance and complicity of the Hellenic cities of Magna Greece and that of the belligerent Samnites, eternal enemies of Rome. While it would have been a good plan during the First Punic War, but was not feasible in the Second.

2. The eventuality of a land invasion of Italy was most unlikely. The Carthaginians could have opened up a passage along the Gallic coast. This offered the advantage of being able to drive a large army, but it had the disadvantage that the Masaliotas and the Roman army itself had several very advantageous positions from which to block the advancing enemy.

It was a very risky route. When Hannibal sent Mutines downriver along the Rodano to stop the Roman cavalry, his Numidians suffered a grave defeat, evidence of the risks involved in allowing the Romans to fight on home ground.

3. It was also possible to disembark in Liguria to avoid being blocked on the land route, but the forces sent could not be very large and, although they could count on the help of the Ligurians, there was the possibility that they could be defeated by the legions before receiving reinforcements.

Curiously, when Hannibal left Italy, to assist the motherland, the Carthaginian troops that remained in Liguria and Gallic Cisalpine resisted the Romans brilliantly for years, mixing with the warriors from local tribes.

4. Finally for the Roman tacticians, from a theoretical point of view, there was another possibility: That someone would drive an army northwards to invade Italy by crossing the Alps. But this was not credible. It was purely and simply impossible!

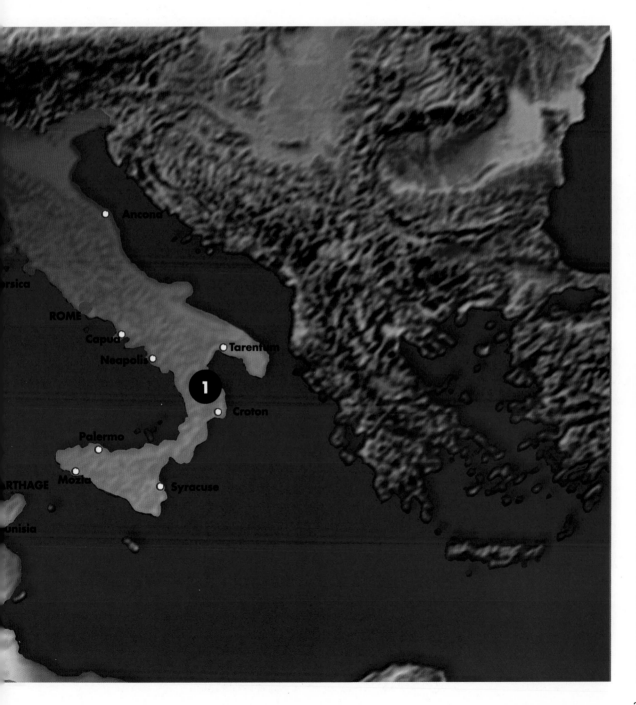

CROSSING THE ALPS

Hannibal left all his army's heavy equipment in Hannon's hands in South Gaul. Hannon was a trusted officer encharged with commanding the troops that were not to follow him into Italy. The Carthaginian leader's calculation was very interesting. As the territory through which he was to pass would be about to collect the harvest, it is unlikely that his men would go hungry and the provisions carried could be kept to a minimum, thus gaining speed. Between the Pyrenees and Rodano, the Carthaginian troops met with little opposition; the pacts with tribal chiefs and exchange of presents facilitated the march without too many incidents. Nevertheless, on arrival at Rodano matters became complicated, as some of the tribes of the region were not willing to let Hannibal's expedition cross to the eastern side of the river. Faced with this situation, he sent part of his cavalry northwards to search for a suitable crossing point, while the task of building river-crossing barges continued on the western shore. The Volscos, the Celtic tribe of the region, with which they maintained good relations, provided the rest of the boats.

Meanwhile, the troops sent north, mostly Celt-Iberians, discovered a fort on an island in the middle of the river, situated less that 30 km from where the bulk of the Punic army was located. They crossed the river with the help of inflated animal skins. After moving south, they placed themselves near the Gallic camp and gave a signal with a bonfire so that Hannibal would know that his men were ready. Having received the message, Hannibal ordered his men to cross to the other side. The Gauls, observing the manoeuvre, got ready to oppose them and spread out along the riverbank. It was at that moment that the Hispanic warriors, in hiding close to the Gallic camp, launched themselves upon the camp and set fire to it. Terrorised, the Gauls began to retreat and soon fled. The whole army could then cross over to the eastern shore, though not without problems, which meant that the Carthaginian engineers had to find a solution for transporting the provisions and the elephants to the other side. After much difficulty, they finally achieved their objective.

During the days that it took for everyone, and everything to cross the river, Hannibal's troops took advantage of the situation to rest and recover. But there was a problem: The Roman fleet was in the allied city of Marseille and Publio Cornelio Scipio, the old one was there with his entire consular army; they had received the news that Hannibal had crossed the Pyrenees and was to be found in South Gaul. After landing, he allowed his troops to rest

A view of the Alps, the mountain range over which Hannibal led his army.

Hannibal crossing the Alps by the Spanish master, Francisco Goya.
Private collection.

foothills of the Alps at the beginning of November 218 BC. In the flat area, Hannibal's cavalry and their Gallic allies could have avoided any hostile element, but in the high mountains, things were different. They suffered from Gallic attacks, avalanches, blocked routes and ice and snow, but after nine days of marching, they reached the highest point of the pass and as the army waited two days for the stragglers, it rested. The descent was difficult and the troops were tired and demoralised; they had suffered all kinds of natural disaster from avalanches blocking their path to snow so deep that it was almost impossible for the elephants to proceed. However, Hannibal's ingenuity, skill and sheer force of personality made it possible for the army to continue the advance. After several more days, they finally reached the area where the snow had not settled and the animals could graze. Three days later, they arrived on the plains. Polibio says that Hannibal took fifteen days to cross the Alps, but it is not known whether he was speaking of the final pass or the entire journey. In any case, the army had suffered much but had finally reached its objective. Hannibal was in Italy.

for several days, so that they would be ready for the inevitable confrontation. A few days later, news arrived that left the consul stupefied: Hannibal was in Rodano. Immediately, three hundred of the finest Roman horsemen, local scouts and a mercenary force of Gauls hired by Masaliotas, went north to locate the bulk of the Punic army. Hannibal, who knew of Scipio's arrival at Marseille, sent a contingent of five hundred Numidians under Mutines to evaluate the situation. The clash took place when the forces met and the Roman heavy cavalry were victorious, killing 300 Numidians at the cost of around 140 men. After locating Hannibal and his army's camp, they returned to inform the consul. Scipio left all the heavy material and provisions that could slow their advance and went to meet Hannibal, but he arrived three days too late. Faced with a lack of material and equipment, he decided not to pursue Hannibal and, after returning to Marseille, he headed for the north of Italy to take control of the forces of the zone, sending the bulk of his troops to Spain, a strategic decision that in hindsight would be crucial in the war.

Even today, the exact route taken by Hannibal is still under debate because there are several historical versions of events and the Romans were probably not even sure of it in Hannibal's time. What is known is that after following the river Rodano northwards, Hannibal reached the

The Carthaginian general leading his troops. In the background can be seen the tightly packed column of troops during their arduous march. War elephants are also shown in the column.

TESINO, TREBIA AND LAKE TRASIMENE

When the news was received that Hannibal's army was in Italy, a wave of terror swept through Rome. The first measure to be adopted was ordering the army stationed on Sicily to return, in preparation for it to be sent against Carthage itself. The best troops that were about to embark for Spain under the command of Publio Cornelio Scipio 'the old one' were also available to confront the threat. The first important battle took place on the banks of the river Tesino, when a force of Roman cavalry, under Scipio, was surprised, ambushed and routed by the better-organized Carthaginian cavalry. Scipio himself was wounded and only the intervention of his son, then a young tribune, saved his life. After retreating to the other side of the River Po, the Romans fortified the banks of the river Trebia with trenches, to await the two legions of Consul Tiberio Sempronio Longo that were advancing by forced march from the south.

Hannibal, as usual, had carried out a detailed analysis of the personalities of the two Roman commanders and knew that the impulsive Sempronio would be unable to tolerate the affront of being challenged without responding. Little by little, he provoked skirmishes with the advance Roman units, from which the Carthaginians always backed down, giving Sempronio a false sense of superiority. Furthermore, knowing that the two consuls took turns in command, he decided to act one day when the aggressive Sempronio was in charge. At night, he sent two thousand men under the command of his brother Magon to occupy secure positions between the streams near the Roman camp and, at daybreak, launched his Numidian cavalry against the Romans and called them to withdraw when the Romans responded. Seeing the apparent success, Sempronio decided to send the bulk of his legions against Hannibal. His men had not eaten breakfast and had to cross icy river streams, soon getting soaking wet so that they were weakened by cold and hunger by the time they reached the Punic lines. The Numidians enticed the Romans to a favourable position and unleashed their cavalry upon them and then later threw themselves on the legions flanks. The majority of the Roman troops apparently felt they had nothing to fear and advanced energetically until reaching the point designated by Hannibal, who then ordered his brother's men to turn and attack the Romans. Fresh and rested, the Carthaginians crushed the Roman defence, whose soldiers were pushed towards the icy waters of the Trebia, where they fell exhausted with most of them drowning from the cold and the weight of their armour. The Romans lost 20,000 men while Hannibal demonstrated once again his great tactical skill.

Scipio, meanwhile, had managed to extract part of the army to Piacenza and a snowstorm hid him from his Carthaginian pursuers; Hannibal acted quite slowly in the persecution, something quite usual throughout the campaign, which occasionally prevented him from exploiting his great victories and his overwhelming tactical superiority. However, his triumph had a spectacular effect among the Gallic tribes of the region, whose men joined his army en-masse. Faced with the hard winter, the Carthaginian tactician decided to make camp and fortify. The ensuing snow and ice killed all the elephants that had survived the Alpine crossing, except for one.

During the winter, Rome recruited eleven new legions and placed the new, immense army under the command of the consuls Cneo Servilio Gemino and Cayo Flaminio. In order to surprise them, Hannibal decided to cross a swampy zone that the Romans felt was impossible. The march itself was terrible and hundreds of men were lost through fever and infections; a high number of animals of burden were also lost. Hannibal himself lost an eye due to an infection. However, his army had made a spectacular advance into the heart of Italy.

Flaminio met his troops, some 25,000 men including two Roman Legions and allied troops at Arezzo, while Gemino met with another two legions at Rimini. The Roman idea was simple and ultimately successful. Between the two armies, they covered any route that

Italian oil painting that shows the passage of Lake Trasimene, site of one of Hannibal's great victories.

Hannibal might choose to take and they only had to inform each other at the first sight of the Punics so that the other army could come to its aid. But, as always, Hannibal knew his enemies' characters very well and tempted the most impulsive of the two, Flaminio, who years earlier had defeated the Insubros. He found it difficult to tolerate a provocation. Hence, Hannibal drove his troops towards his army, setting fire to harvests and villages, destroying everything. When the educated Flaminio pursued him, he withdrew to Lake Trasimene and waited. At daybreak on the 21st July 217 BC, the Roman cavalry that had gone ahead to monitor the enemy's movements informed Flaminio that Hannibal was breaking camp. Imagining that the Carthaginian was going to escape him, he set off in pursuit, advancing along the length of the lakeshore through the mist, unaware that the majority of the enemy troops were posted in the wooded slopes next to the lake. At Hannibal's signal, the air was filled with the sound of the horns and trumpets of the Gauls, Spanish, Liby-Phoenicians and Numidians, who charged downhill against the unprepared legions. Trapped in the worst possible situation, with the lake behind them and unable to deploy effectively, the legionaries were destroyed. Valiantly, some groups of

Fragment of a Carthaginian triumphal monument discovered in Tunisia. It shows chain mail, the armour of Celtic origin as highly valued by the Romans as by the Punic.

Romans retreated into the lake, where they were dragged down by the weight of their armour. Flaminio fell fighting ferociously against the Insubro Gauls that he had almost wiped out years before and who now had the opportunity to exact their revenge. Fifteen thousand legionaries and allies perished, fighting to the end; another ten thousand were held prisoner. The whole Roman army was destroyed.

After this disaster, the Urban Praetor of Rome, supreme magistrate in the absence of the consuls, called together the people and gave them the terrible news: "We have been defeated in a great battle". It was not to be the last misfortune. Gemino's cavalry of four thousand men had tried to join Flaminio to reinforce his troops but, as usual, he too fell into a perfect Carthaginian ambush and the cavalry was massacred.

Hannibal had demonstrated stunning tactical superiority over the legions in a very short space of time. Rome had suffered three consecutive defeats but, as with Pirro, Hannibal now saw how the Romans refused to negotiate any kind of peace. The war was to continue. If the great Punic leader wanted to triumph, he would have to inflict a defeat upon Rome so overwhelming that it would provoke, once and for all, an uprising of the oppressed people of Italy.

Lake Trasimene was Hannibal's finest example of a classic ambush. He used all the enemies' weaknesses, the cavalry's lack of reconnaissance to the Roman general's lack of energy, to lure the Roman legions into a deathtrap.

After the defeat at Lake Trasimene, the Senate named Quinto Fabio Maximo dictator, awarding him full powers to face the fearful Hannibal. The choice was very appropriate. Fabio had great military experience and was used to extended campaigns with large forces, which enabled him to quickly detect what Hannibal's real weak point was: his own army.

Hannibal had 50,000 men permanently stationed in Italy, which implied the need to maintain provisions and control key points in the occupied territory, but there was something else. The Etruscans, wary after years of defeat by the Romans, had not joined forces with him; hence Hannibal continued to move through enemy territory and needed more arms, food and beasts of burden. Logistics were Hannibal's Aquilles heel. If the Romans could manage to isolate him from his sources of provisions, he would die like a fish out of water.

Astutely, Fabio began to isolate the Carthaginians, attacking his solitary and left-behind units and even almost managing to play a trick on the king of ambush, Hannibal himself. However, unfortunately for both Fabio and Rome, their enemies in the Senate, who were almost all landholding aristocracy with their lands occupied saw themselves losing income. They

Mosaic from the 2nd Century BC discovered in Italy. It is one of the oldest representations of the Republican Legions. They used muscular cuirasses and plate mail. Their helmets carried large crests without feathers. All had decorated shields. Tens of thousands of men similar to these were massacred at Cannae.

Hannibal and Scipio meet face to face. Generals in those times usually had a rendezvous before the battle to negotiate a possible peaceful surrender. Usually this was a mere formality.

revoked most of Fabio's powers and forced him to accept a decisive battle, mocking his prudence and accusing him of cowardess.

Hence, after the six months of command awarded by law to dictators, in spite of the evident success of the fabiana tactics that were seriously damaging Hannibal, two new consuls were elected, Cayo Terencio Varrón and Lucio Emilio Paulo, who had previously pleaded for direct combat against the Carthaginians. In charge of the largest army that Rome had ever seen, they headed south in search of Hannibal, oblivious to what was about to transpire.

As well as the two consuls, the Roman army had two pro-consuls, Cneo Servilio Gemino and Marco Minucio Rufo, who replaced the deceased Flaminio. Like the two consuls, they were experienced soldiers but not very imaginative. They commanded Roman Legions and knew that it was very difficult to win a battle against a Roman army, hence they relied more on

Combat between a Roman cavalryman and a Numidian of the Carthaginian army.

their own skill and the product of the 'system' than on the need to rely on an army of loyal, capable, well-trained and motivated men. Furthermore, there was another problem, they had learnt nothing from the lessons of the disasters at Tesino, Trebia and Lake Trasimene and had no understanding of whom they were up against.

The overwhelming Carthaginian victory at Cannae wasn't enough to retain control of the Mediterranean. This was determined at the battle of Zama. A detail of a painting by Tintoretto.

Italian breastplates probably used by Hannibal's mercenaries during the Punic Wars. They were made of two bronze plates held at the shoulders and waist with leather straps.

With respect to Hannibal, he was left with only one choice in that summer of 216 BC, to secure a decisive victory that would either force Rome to sue for peace or to destroy her allies. To achieve this he had to destroy the Roman army at any cost, although he knew it would be no easy task. How was he to defeat, on the open battlefield, an army twice the size of his own and, moreover, well armed and equipped?

To some extent, the Roman strategy was the mirror opposite; to force the Carthaginians to fight a decisive battle, a fight in which both sides would place all their bets on a single card. Fabio's strategy may seem correct to us today, but for the Romans at the time it was exasperating and a whole series of political, economic and even moral factors led the Roman army towards what the leaders desired: a great battle. The problem for them was that this was also what Hannibal wanted.

On the 2nd of August 216 BC, both armies met face-to-face on the plain near the small town of Cannae. The terrain was perfect for the Romans, or at least that was what their commander's thought. It was as flat as the palm of a hand, between the River Aufidio and the hill on which Cannae was located. The Romans had converted Cannae into a supply base; the legions could have blocked the whole area between the river and the hill, but instead they decided to allow the enemy cavalry to spread out, acting in the 'usual' fashion, dispersing their own cavalry at the wings and maintaining a compact block of infantry. The problem was that acting in the 'usual' fashion was a very fool-hardy decision when faced with Hannibal.

THE GREATEST VICTORY
CANNAE, 2ND OF AUGUST 216 BC.

The Battle of Cannae has had an enormous influence on military treatises and on Western tactical doctrine throughout history for one simple reason: it was the perfect victory.

War in the 3rd Century BC.

It is generally strange that a good general should wish to risk everything in a single battle. However, due to the fate of destiny, this is what the Roman consuls and the great Hannibal chose to do on that hot summer day in the year 216 BC, leading their armies into the greatest battle of ancient times and one of the most impressive, if not the most impressive in history.

Losses in classical battles were low, about 5%, a very small percentage by modern standards, but certain facts are usually overlooked: The tense emotion and stress of fighting with bladed weapons and the ensuing fatigue meant that there were few real moments of continual combat. After an exchange of projectiles, the armies had to meet at close quarters, something that was very difficult to insist if they were not well-trained and possessed great determination and courage. None of this happened at Cannae.

Hannibal's losses in the battle, around 15%, were abnormally high, but were nothing compared to the blood-chilling 65% or more of the Romans and their allies.

Phase 1: Prior actions

Both armies spread out along the plain facing each other. The two consular armies united with the four Apulian legions to form a seemingly overwhelming force. In total, eight Roman legions and the eight Latin units must have been an imposing sight, spread out with their 80,000 infantry and 6400 horsemen.

In the first rank, there were 10 hastati, the youngest soldiers. Behind, there were 10 principes, veterans in the prime of life and behind them 10 experienced triarii. Spread out behind them was the velites, light infantry.

Hannibal adopted a strange formation, placing his Gallic and Spanish infantry units in mixed groups, dividing the African phalange into two groups to the left and right of the half moon. After initial skirmishing between the wings of the light infantry in which the efficient Balearic slingers gained a wide advantage, the clash of the two infantries began.

Meanwhile, the Numidian cavalry attained a clear success against the allied heavy cavalry, something apparently incredible for the time even with the odds of just over two to one. The Carthaginian, Spanish and Gallic heavy cavalry of Hasdrubal, with its six thousand horsemen, annihilated the two thousand six hundred Romans with great ease.

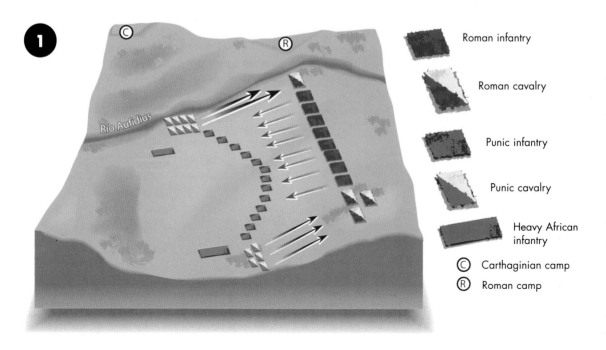

1

Río Aufidius

Ⓒ Carthaginian camp
Ⓡ Roman camp

Roman infantry

Roman cavalry

Punic infantry

Punic cavalry

Heavy African infantry

Phase 2: The Crisis

Slowly and relentlessly, the Roman infantry was squeezed by the crescent formed by the Gauls and Spanish pressing them inexorably in. Nonetheless, the Roman formation was so dense in such a restricted space, that the legions could use their full force, although the pressure was immense. Situated behind his men, Hannibal urged them on although confronted with a difficult situation.

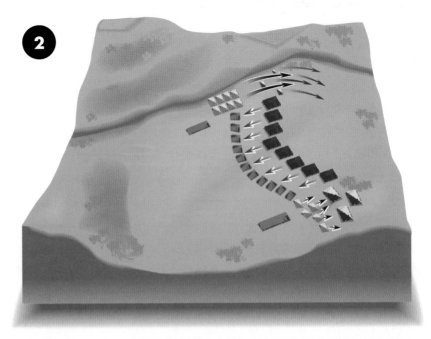

After hours of battle, the Roman pressure finally broke the crescent and, at first appearance, it seemed that the fragile Spanish and Gallic lines would disintegrate at any moment. However, this was not to be. Just when the situation appeared desperate, the African phalanges closed in on the Roman flanks that had taken over their position. Their frightful six-metre lances presented an unexpected threat to the legions. Finally, the Carthaginian cavalry, Numidians, Gauls and Spanish, attacked the legions from behind. The Roman's own impetuousness had driven them into a trap.

Once the pressure of the legionaries had been relieved, the persecuted Spanish and Gallic troops recovered and closed ranks. Compressed into an ever-shrinking area, the Romans could hardly move and suffocated under the intense summer heat and the weight of their weapons and cuirasses.

Phase 3: The final

Once they had surrounded the Roman troops there was no escape. At that moment, the longest phase of the battle began, lasting for hours and in which the Liby-Phoenician, Numidian, Celt-Iberian, Gallic and Iberian warriors just killed and killed in an orgy of collective ecstasy and blood lust until they could kill no more. Trapped and unable to escape, without space to move, the legionaries still did not surrender and fought to the bitter end, displaying magnificent, foolhardy courage. Hannibal's men worked in shifts, retiring to rest before returning to continue the carnage. It is calculated that more than 100,000 litres of blood were spilt over just a few square kilometres of ground in a single day. Once the blood lust had been expended, tens of thousand of men lay dead amid the dust, mud and blood. Hannibal had achieved the greatest victory in history.

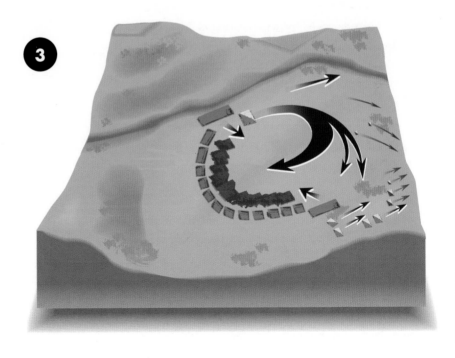

HANNIBAL'S DILEMMA

When everything had finished at Cannae, both the victorious and the defeated were in a dazed stupor. The first night on the battlefield, in spite of the desperate fatigue, the survivors began to realise what had transpired. The largest army in the history of Rome had simply ceased to exist. Paulo, Servilio and Minucio had all fallen fighting, together with the two consuls, eight members of the senatorial census and 50,000 legionaries. A mere 10,000 men were taken prisoner. The Roman base camp surrendered without a fight, overwhelmed by the unthinkable.

When the news reached Rome, panic struck and the terrified population prepared themselves for the worst. The Senate, however, remained calm. It freed and armed slaves and criminals, mobilising practically the whole population. Talk of suing for peace was banned under penalty of death and everything was made available for a fight without quarter. For generations after, the Romans would remember with pride how their predecessors had refused to surrender or even negotiate with their country's invaders. While, in the long term, their consistency and steadfastness was rewarded, there was still ten days left until the inevitable terrible clash. The Roman citizen's will to resist and willingness to fight were an inspiration.

It is said that Hannibal himself arrived at the walls of Rome and was dismayed, perhaps thinking of the smaller Saguntum that resisted him for eight months. He thought that his army would be unable to take the city. This was undoubtedly Hannibal's most controversial decision. His cavalry general said: "You know how to win, Hannibal, but you don't know what to do with your victories". All his detractors have made this harsh judgement of Hannibal and the truth is… they were right! It is possible that Hannibal didn't stand much chance of subduing Rome. After all, he had lost a large percentage of his troops at Cannae, much more than was usual for a battle of the period, and he was also aware that he couldn't take the city in a short space of time. He had neither siege weapons nor the means to manufacture them and that's where it is believed he made his mistake. Whatever the outcome, he had to take the risk; the goddess of war rewards those who take risks and, after all, if he wasn't willing to make such as decision, why did he go to Italy in the first place? After Cannae and his refusal to attack Rome, Hannibal's expedition became a simple adventure. The truth is…it was never more than that!

However, at first, the facts appeared to prove that Hannibal was correct. The overwhelming defeat at Cannae ended up dividing the Italian allied forces. The defections in Southern and Central Italy were notable and a substantial part of the people of the region united with the Carthaginians. Samnites, Brutii, Lucanians and the major cities of Magna Greece enthusiastically joined forces with Hannibal. In 212 BC, Tarento, the city over which the Pirro War was fought, fell into the hands of Hannibal and, shortly after, he captured Capua, one of the richest areas of Italy. The war had changed dramatically for Rome. Hannibal now dominated Campania, Italy's granary, and didn't need to roam in search of food. The Appian Way, the most important of those constructed by the Romans was now cut off.

Three Latin warriors. A mounted Lucanian horseman. The cavalry from the Campania region, in the South of Italy, was the finest in the Peninsula and the Romans had benefited greatly from the experience. Armed with a mixture of Latin, Greek and even Celtic styles, the Latin defection could have caused mortal damage to Rome in other times, but by the close of the 3rd Century BC, it was evident that the majority of the population saw much greater risks in challenging the might of Rome.

The other two warriors are Samnites. During decades of the 4th Century BC and until the Battle of Sentinum (293 BC) they were Rome's bitterest enemies. Even as late as the 1st Century BC, during the Social War, the Samnite, Poncio Telesino, called Rome "the refuge of the devouring wolf of the people of Italy". The hatred between both peoples was all consuming. However, during the Second Punic War, the Samnite fighting spirit was finally broken. Although they have been represented with their traditional accoutrements, feathered helmets, short tunics, shields and javelins, it is possible that after years of fighting, the Romans had adapted to their style of combat and used heavy armour.

HANNIBAL AD PORTAS

When the Romans were confronted with the terrible dilemma of having lost a substantial and important part of their territory, they reacted in their usual manner... with energy and decision. By fighting a war of attrition on the frontiers of Sicily and Spain during which the Punic armies were systematically destroyed, they were able to prevent them assisting Hannibal.

In Italy, Hannibal had just one strategy: force the Italianate peoples to defect and oblige Rome to surrender. This he did not achieve and time continued to pass. The same thing that had happened at Sicily in the First War was to be repeated in Italy in the Second. The Romans initiated an exhausting war of attrition. By utilising their enormous resources and taking the opportunity to train their inexperienced troops, they limited themselves to taking fortified positions such as isolated hill cities, protecting their isolated points, now in enemy territory and to vigorously attack the people who had abandoned the alliance. For years, there were hardly any set battles; fighting was limited to sordid and hard campaigns in the mountains and hills. The Romans didn't offer Hannibal the opportunity to fight a decisive battle while continuing to arm and equip new troops.

Desperate, because he didn't achieve any decisive victories, only a few minor ones while trying to avoid the harassment to which his allies in Capua were subjected, he tried a surprising diversionary manoeuvre and advanced on Rome. The march took place at surprising speed and they were shortly camped before her walls. Rome, however, was no longer in the same situation as in 216 BC. It was well fortified and defended and knew that it could find auxiliary troops at short notice. In consequence, Hannibal's threat rapidly dissipated. The following year, 211 BC, the Romans assumed positions at Capua and recaptured it. Little by little, Carthage's allies returned to

Rome's thrall. Rome had also rediscovered the Fabian tactic, which gave them such good results in so little time that the tactics were applied and Hannibal felt more and more threatened. Nevertheless, while he still had ports in his hands, he could have received help from Carthage, which did little for him, or Macedonia that was now also at war with the Romans.

In 209 BC, Tarento fell, the finest trophy ever captured by Hannibal, which demonstrated once and for all that the Carthaginians could not fight off more that one Roman attack at a time. However, by sheer force of personality, genius and tremendous tactical skill, Hannibal continued to be a formidable rival. In 212 BC, he had inflicted a terrible defeat at Herdonea on the Praetor, Cneo Fluvio Flaco, who was slain in an ambush identical to that at Trebia while also losing 16,000 men. In 209 BC, Cneo Fluvio Centumalo suffered a similar defeat in almost the same spot, leaving 13,000 men on the field. Rome, however, continued to resist.

In 207 BC, Hasdrubal, defeated in Spain, had managed to open up a passage to Italy, following his elder brother's route and reaching his objective. After years of desperate war against Hannibal, the Romans were now faced with a second Carthaginian army, also land-based. Although isolated in the south of the peninsula, Hannibal remained unconquered and it was imperative that the Romans prevent the recent arrivals from joining them at any cost. Fortunately for Rome, things were not the same as in 218 BC and the Roman army had learnt many lessons. On 22nd June 207 BC, the troops under

The famous fresco of Paestum, in Lucania. It represents Samnite warriors, Rome's bitterest enemies in the 4th Century BC; they were yet to unite with Hannibal, but by then, his power was broken.

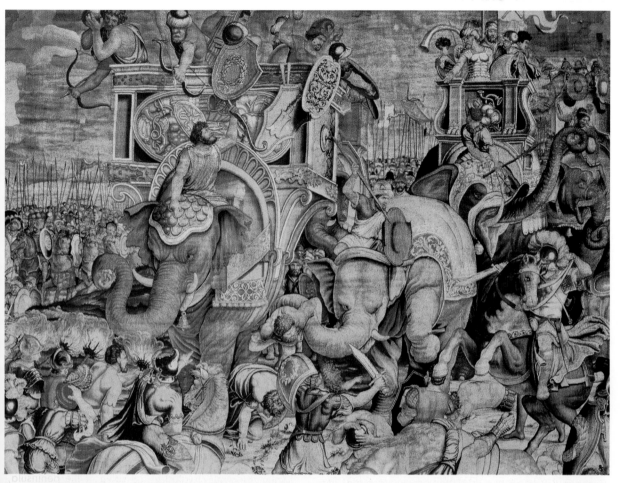

The Battle of Zama as depicted in a 16th Century tapestry in the Royal Palace, Madrid. After years of fighting and having received hardly any news from Carthage, Hannibal was called to defend his homeland at a crucial moment.

Pictorial representation of a Samnite warrior.

the joint command of Marco Livio Salinator and Cayo Claudio Neron, confronted the Carthaginians on the Metaurus and gained a decisive victory. Hasdrubal himself was slain during the battle.

In 205 BC, Magon, Hannibal's younger brother, landed 12,000 infantry and 2,000 cavalry at Genova. His army had a very high proportion of Balearics and, furthermore, shortly afterwards received from Carthage a further 7 elephants, 6,000 infantry, 800 cavalry and sufficient funds to hire Ligurians. In spite of two years intensive fighting in the region, he never managed to efficiently back up his brother's actions, and was, moreover, never be able to link up with him. In 203 BC, the praetor, Publio Quinctilio Varo, and the pro-consul, Marco Cornelio Cetego, with their four legions forced him to give battle in Gallic Insubro territory. Magon's lines were destroyed and he was wounded in the leg. While recovering from his wounds, he received orders from Carthage to return to his homeland, but he died on the return journey.

ZAMA, 202 BC.

Elected Consul in 205 BC, Scipio Africanus 'the African', asked for permission for a direct assault on Carthage. The expedition set off the following year and after landing in Africa, easily defeated the few troops they met during their advance. Furthermore, and fortunately for him, the Numidian King Masinissa joined the Romans. After blockading Utica, Scipio comprehensively defeated all the troops sent against him and provisioned his Castra Cornelio fort with a reserve of food, livestock and beasts of burden. For the remainder of the year, Scipio continued without respite. He defeated the North African Punic Army and the Numidians of Syphax, Carthage's most important ally. This ensured that the Punic Senate and the Peace Party gained popularity over those who wanted to continue the war. Finally, negotiations were opened with Scipio and his demands were accepted in order to gain time until Hannibal returned. He abandoned Italy and returned to the homeland where he was a stranger. Upon his arrival, Hannibal spent some time organising the army and preparing it for the coming battle.

Both forces finally met close to the town of Zama. The Romans had their camp near the city that Polibio called Magaron. Their position was good and they also had access to an adequate water supply. The Carthaginians, meanwhile, also occupied an excellent position, somewhat better than the Roman's, but with no nearby water supply. The following day the commanders opened negotiations and, on the day after, both armies took up their battle positions on the battlefield. There were hardly any preliminary skirmishes, evidence of both groups' desire for battle. It is suggested that the Romans had slightly less infantry but more cavalry, although Appian's numbers are not reliable.

Scipio positioned the Roman and Italian cavalry on the left under Lelio's command, with Masinissa's Numidian cavalry on the right, the legions in the centre and the alae, in their usual triplex acies formation, but with a subtle variation. Instead of placing the principes to cover the gaps between the hastate, he placed them behind and then, behind them, went the triari. This formation left large 'corridors' that were covered by groups of velites.

Hannibal held 80 elephants in reserve and placed his Numidians in front of those of Masinissa with the remaining cavalry in front of Lelio. In the centre were three infantry units, one with the rest of Magon's Army-Gauls, Ligurians, some Africans and Balearics, another with Liby-Phoenicians and citizens of Carthage and, finally, the Italian veterans with their chain mail and Roman shields. The idea that Macedonians were present is almost certainly a myth.

The battle was bitterly fought and difficult. The elephants caused mayhem and, although Hannibal's troops fought well, the Roman Army showed remarkable discipline and was capable of completely reorganising itself on the actual battlefield. The battle was finally resolved by Lelio's cavalry, which attacked Hannibal's veterans from behind. While Hannibal's basic plan was a good one, it was Scipio's abilities as a general coupled with the high morale and fighting capability of the legionaries that ensured a Carthaginian defeat.

A mounted Hannibal issuing instructions to his troops. The Punic general is mounted on a horse protected by a bronze cuirass for defence against infantry. He is wearing a lined cuirass reinforced with metal plates to ward off cuts and blows.

The officer beside him is a veteran of the Italian campaign and is wearing chain mail, like the greater part of the Carthaginian infantry. During the years of war in Europe, the chain mail was tested for functionality and efficiency. His weapon, although appearing to be an Iberian falcate, is in fact a kopis or machaira, a Greek weapon widely used by the cavalry. The other mounted officer, unlike the first, is an inexperienced youth who has never been on campaign away from Carthage. His uniform is more traditional and befitting of the upper class that constituted the Carthaginian oligarchy.

LIFE AS A FUGITIVE

Following the Zama defeat, Carthage sued for peace. The Roman conditions, drafted by Scipio, were onerous. All the elephants were confiscated and Carthage was allowed just ten battleships. It retained its African territory, but lost all its maritime possessions. The Numidian kingdom of Masinissa was considerably expanded. On top of all this, a punitive tribute of 10,000 talents of silver a year was imposed for a period of 50 years.

Finally, the Carthaginians had to maintain the Roman Army for three months and pay them until the ratification of the treaty arrived. This occurred in the spring of 201 BC, when the Senate of Rome accepted Scipio's conditions and set everything in place to carry out the agreement.

Hannibal served in the position of commander-in-chief of the Carthaginian Army for several years and, in 196 BC, was elected judge. This saw the onset of his conflict with the Counsel of the One Hundred and Four and various judges of the oligarchy whom he accused of diverting public funds. He demonstrated that the city was rich and efficient enough that it could pay the debt to Rome simply by controlling and eliminating corruption. While this reinforced his power in the Popular Assembly, it cost him the enmity of the oligarchy and his political adversaries. These reported him to Rome, accusing him of conspiring with Antiochus III. While Scipio opposed the measures against Hannibal, he couldn't prevent a commission being sent to Carthage to deal with the accusations. Wary of his enemies' power, Hannibal fled to the Court of Antioch, first passing through Tyre, Carthage's motherland.

Hannibal's brief rule laid the foundations of Carthage's return to prosperity, such that it managed to pay the fifty-year debt to Rome in just 10 years, though Rome would have preferred them to fulfil the treaty to remind them of their defeat. The great Carthaginian general didn't live to see this success. He led a fleet from Antioch in the war against Rome, always trying to convince them to invade Italy. After the new Roman victory, he escaped to Bitinia, in 183 BC, where he took refuge in the court of King Prusias, for whom he won a surprising naval battle against the Pergamo fleet.

The Romans relentlessly pursued Hannibal and pressured the Bitinian king not to assist him. The monarch sent soldiers to Hannibal's house where, unable to escape, he decided to commit suicide by poison. A sad end for one of the greatest warriors of all time.

Scipio Africanus "The African" (235 – 183 BC). A great Roman military leader. He concluded his career by defeating Hannibal's army at Zama.

Meeting at Efeso.

Legend states that the Hellenic city was rediscovered by Hannibal and Scipio. The Roman general formed part of a delegation sent to King Antiochus III during the time that Hannibal was taking refuge in his court. It is said that the Roman asked the Punic general:

—Who are the greatest generals of history?

To which the Carthaginian replied:

—Alexander the Great, Pirro and I

Perhaps, surprised by the reply, Scipio then asked him:

—And if you had won at Zama?

To which Hannibal replied:

—In that case, I would have put myself in the first position.

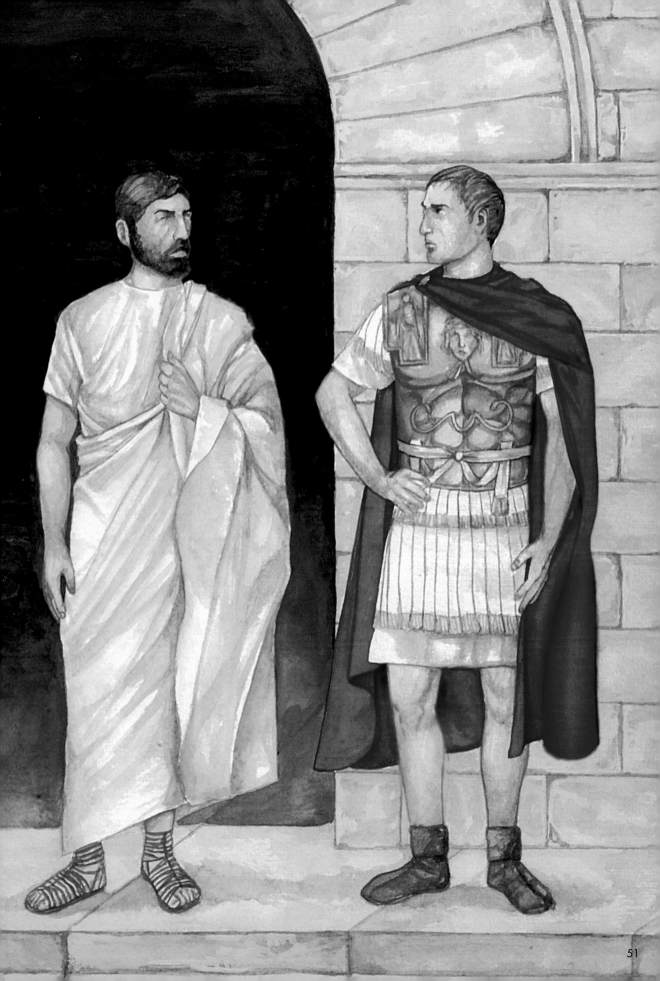